NAMES WITH A
PROMISE

WRITTEN BY KATHRYN TALPOS

Founder of Abiding Love Co.

Names with a Promise: A Study and Prayer Guide of the Names of God

Published by Burning Soul Press

Paperback: 978-1-964924-16-8
Ebook: 978-1-964924-17-5

Table of Contents

Introduction

In Jewish tradition, you'll find names carry a purpose beyond parental preference. Throughout the Bible, you can read name after name that has a purposeful, and very often prophetic, meaning behind it. A name carried a personal meaning for parents, an understanding of the job or role a child was destined for, or even the personality they would be known for.

Similarly, God has countless names highlighting His characteristics, promises, and the experiences His people have with Him. Each name holds a unique perspective into one of the many aspects of who God is; a place He wishes to open Himself up to us. These names reveal a power that many do not tap into - the testimonies and promises that are available to each one of us. The names of God come with a promise that we can also experience Him in these same facets.

Names with a Promise is written to share these names along with guided prayers for you to intentionally grow closer to God, taking hold of the promise each one brings for your own life and asking God to reveal Himself to you personally in these facets.

> *These names reveal a power that many do not tap into - the testimonies and promises that are available to each one of us.*

WEEK ONE

01 Elohim: God the Creator

> "In the beginning, God created the heavens and the earth." (Genesis 1:1)

The first thing we learn about God is that He is the ultimate creator. He speaks things into life with His very words - His definition of beauty, perfection, and creativity is unparalleled to anything we can imagine. After creating the awe-inspiring planet we live in *(and don't forget all of space!)* - all the mountains, seas, animals, and seasons - Elohim, the Creator, still had more in His mind... *you.*

In Genesis 1:26, Elohim created humanity in His image. He described all He had created prior as "good," but when He made you - His ultimate creation - He said it was "very good" (v. 31). As a potter molds the clay, so Elohim molded us, each unique, purposeful, and equally precious in His eyes.

As Elohim's creation, we're also made to create. We are commanded to be fruitful and multiply *(that isn't just about making babies!)*. We have the opportunity to create with whatever talents we have for God's glory. We have the honor to use our gifts of creativity to bring glory to the ultimate Creator. What a beautiful truth it is that we were formed on purpose and for a purpose - *we are anything but a mistake.*

Praying Over the Promises of His Names

The next page has a prayer to Elohim, God the Creator. Use the lines provided to create your own personal prayer.

Elohim,

Psalm 139 tells me that you have intentionally woven and created me in my mother's womb. It is not a mistake that I was made with these specific talents, dreams, desires, and skills.

As your child, made in your image, you call me to create just like you. In this time with you today, I ask that you would refresh me with your creativity and refill me with a vision and passion to use what you've given me. I want to create something beautiful that brings glory and honor to you. Awaken me with new dreams. Fill me with unique ideas for how to share who you are with the world. Show me how to refine my skills and increase my work ethic so that everything I create shows great skill and precision.

Let me be like Bezalel in Exodus 31:1-6, who was created for a specific purpose. As you equipped him with the vision, skill, support, and supplies needed to build your Tabernacle, do the same for me - filling me with vision - so that I may lead others to encounter you with what I create!

Ways to Make this Prayer Personal:	1	2	3
	Have a dream or something God has given you vision to create? Ask for wisdom and direction to make it happen!	Are you burnt out and struggling with creativity? Ask Holy Spirit to reawaken your creativity.	Ask for help to practice and refine the talents He has given you so that you can create and bring glory to Him!

_____

_____

_____

_____

_____

_____

02 El Roi: The God Who Sees Me

"She gave this name to the Lord who spoke to her: 'You are the God who sees me,' for she said, 'I have now seen the One who sees me.'" (Genesis 16:13, NIV)

The story of El Roi comes from a God encounter with a young, foreign woman named Hagar. This woman was at the end of the line for who God "should care about." She was a pagan slave of Abraham and Sarah - the woman who later gives birth to the first son of Abraham (outside of the covenant made with God for Isaac).

Given into marriage to Abraham without a choice, Hagar conceives a child and looks upon Sarah with contempt. Outraged, Sarah harshly treats her servant to the point Hagar flees to the wilderness in desperation. I can only imagine Hagar sitting there - defenseless, discouraged, scared, and feeling unloved - left with nowhere to turn. She had no family or friends to support her, and her Egyptian gods had no power to save.

But God - a phrase that never gets old. *But God*, El Roi, is the One who always sees us. He sees us with the care and love of a Good Father; His eyes are filled with a love unlike any other.

He isn't scared off by our imperfections, sins, or problems. El Roi sees us right where we are, but not in a passive way - He sees us in and through all of the situations we experience. He does not simply see and feel bad for us as we struggle. El Roi has the heart of a Father who rushes to the aid of His children when they need Him most. *We are not forgotten.*

In this passage, El Roi comes to find Hagar - a woman who does not know Him yet as the God of Israel. In the middle of her heartbreak, He comes to comfort her in ways no one else could. His sight is beyond the present moment of suffering, and He shares with her the future victory she will have - bringing hope and light into a seemingly hopeless situation.

Sometimes, we think we have to beg God to come into our situations, yet the funny thing about that is El Roi is already there waiting for us. He was in it before we came to that moment, He is in it as we experience it, and He holds our future in His hands - *a promise that no matter how hopeless a situation may seem, He already has a victory waiting for us.*

In the meantime, we cannot shy away from the hard moments; rather, we must turn back to what God has asked us to do, remembering that El Roi is with us.

Do you want to know something interesting about this woman? Hagar is the only person in the Bible to actually name God. Sure, there were people that named stones of remembrance, wells, and other landmarks after God's characteristics, but it was an unknown, foreign slave - a helpless and often forgotten part of the Abraham and Sarah narrative - who was important enough to God to remember. More than that, Hagar and the story she carried were important enough to El Roi to forever document in His Word.

He isn't scared off by our imperfections, sins, or problems. El Roi sees us right where we are, but not in a passive way - He sees us in and through all of the situations we experience.

Praying Over the Promises of His Names

El Roi,

There are days when I feel alone, unnoticed by the world around me. And, when loved ones let me down, I can't help but struggle with feeling unwanted and unloved. I question if I truly matter.

Yet, when these moments come, I choose to remind myself of who you are, El Roi. In your name, I can remind myself that no matter what anyone else does or says, you see me - *you never leave me* - and you love me with an everlasting love. When I'm having a hard time, I know you are the best friend that anyone can have. You will always be there for me when I need you.

The name El Roi holds a promise for me that you are the One who will never leave or forsake me. I'm not unwanted, unloved, or forgotten. You, El Roi, are the Almighty God who created me, knows me intimately, and sees me with the deep love of a Good Father.

Ways to Make this Prayer Personal:

✔ Do you struggle with feeling noticed, loved, or wanted? Perhaps you've been betrayed or let down by someone close to you. If you haven't healed from this (or not yet forgiven those who wronged you), ask God to help you fully forgive and heal from the words spoken about (or to) you or any other actions taken against you. Unforgiveness holds us back - *not the one who hurt us.* Rest in the promise that El Roi sees you in the midst of your pain and has plans to heal and redeem your situation.

✔ Be honest with God about feelings of insecurity. If you have a hard time accepting the love God has for you, ask Him to open your heart and heal you in the areas keeping you from believing this truth. You may not know what a Good Father looks like, but God is full of grace to show you.

_____

_____

_____

_____

_____

03 Jehovah Rapha: Lord our Healer

> "If you will diligently listen to the voice of the Lord your God, and do that which is right in his eyes, and give ear to his commandments and keep all his statutes, I will put none of the diseases on you that I put on the Egyptians, for I am the Lord, your healer." (Exodus 15:26, ESV)

The story of Jehovah Rapha comes right after Moses and the Israelites narrowly escape the Pharaoh through the Red Sea. This chapter begins with the Israelites worshipping God in song for the miracle they experienced. Following this worship set, however, they complain to Moses for clean water, which the Lord supplies through a tree. In verse 25, God puts a test before the people, promising that if they listen and obey His voice and commands, God will be Jehovah Rapha for them.

In the New Testament, we're more acquainted with the name of Jesus, the fulfillment of Isaiah 53:5. Through His piercings on the cross, we are now healed. This Truth is why we can boldly come to the throne of Jehovah Rapha and ask for healing in our body - not just physically, but in our heart, mind, and soul. God delights in healing His people, but we can't forget our part: to seek the Lord and keep His commandments. A sinful world brought illness in the first place, and living obedient to His Word heals and saves us from our fleshly nature.

Praying Over the Promises of His Names

The next page has prayers to Jehovah Rapha for specific areas of healing. Then, create your own prayer in the lines provided.

Jehovah Rapha,

FOR THE MIND

I ask that my mind would be renewed in Your Name. Please heal me from anything sinful I've heard, seen, or experienced. Take any anxiety, depression, dark or suicidal thoughts away and replace it with your light and peace. I pray the blood of Jesus over my mind right now and invite your Holy Spirit to renew me with your Word.

FOR THE HEART

Only you know the pain of my heart. *Jehovah Rapha,* I invite you into my heart and ask you to heal the places you see unhealed hurt, trauma, bitterness, and unforgiveness. Heal me from the words spoken over me (said by myself and others) - replacing the lies, feelings of insufficiency, and burden of anxiety, depression, or any other darkness with your Truth and perfect love that heals all things.

FOR THE BODY

When Jesus died on the cross, His blood was shed so I can be whole. Your Word says that by His stripes, I am healed (Isaiah 53:5; 1 Peter 2:24), so I pray today and ask for your divine healing over my body. May you have the full reward of the price you paid on the cross with complete healing from my head to my toes. In Jesus' Name, I declare that all spirits of infirmity must go. Jehovah Rapha, I ask that you'd realign my body to your will - *full healing and abundant life.*

_____

_____

_____

_____

_____

04 Jehovah Jireh: The Lord will Provide

"Abraham named the place Yahweh-Jireh (which means 'the Lord will provide'). To this day, people still use that name as a proverb: 'On the mountain of the Lord it will be provided.'" (Genesis 22:14)

Abraham waited a long time to receive his promised child. God promised him many things - some of which he died without seeing fully come to pass (Hebrews 11:13). Yet, the arrival of Isaac was a beautiful example of God's faithfulness. I can only imagine how joyful Abraham was to receive his long-awaited promise.

Many years later, this promised child was the very thing God asked him to sacrifice. However, rather than doubt that God would fulfill His covenant, Abraham was obedient to His command. He had full faith that God would provide within His situation, telling his son "God will provide for himself the lamb for a burnt offering."

How often do we doubt the character of God when we face what we see as a lack or are told to sacrifice something precious to us? So easily we can yell "MINE!" and hold onto the things we treasure, yet forget the One who gave it to us in the first place.

God doesn't "hold out" on us or ask us to sacrifice without taking care of us. What matters most to Him is our heart posture - what is most important to us at the end of the day: *our relationship with God or the temporary things of this world?*

When we have our hearts in the right place, we remember that our first priority is God. With that foundation, we have full trust in Jehovah Jireh to take care of every single need we have. At the end of the day, He knows what we need better than we do, so why do we so easily forget that He will provide in the way He knows is the best for us? If He provided to Abraham, His friend, how much more will He provide for His children?

Praying Over the Promises of His Names

Jehovah Jireh,

You are the Lord who provides. You created me, see me, and know me intimately, so I will not fixate on the things I don't have; instead, I will fix my eyes on you and trust your timing. I pray that you will fill every need in my life. Please show yourself, Jehovah Jireh, in my finances, relationships, job, and anywhere else you know I need provision. Bless these areas of my life so that I may use all the things that I have to give glory back to you.

I praise you, for you provide all things. There is not a breath escaping my lungs that does not owe itself to your grace. In the same way, I commit the money in the bank, the food in my fridge, the clothes in my closet, the car in the driveway, the security of my job, and the relationships in my life to you. I humble myself with the reminder that nothing I have was mine to begin with - *everything I am and have is yours.*

Matthew 6:33 says to seek first the Kingdom of God and that all the needs I have will be taken care of. I hold fast to the promise that it is not that you "may" provide, but that you "will" provide. I praise you, Jehovah Jireh, before the provision comes!

_____

_____

_____

_____

_____

_____

05 Yahweh Shalom: Lord is Peace

> "'It is alright,' the Lord replied. 'Do not be afraid. You will not die.' Gideon built an altar to the Lord there and named it Yahweh-Shalom (which means 'the Lord is peace')." (Judges 6:23-24)

Gideon knew a thing or two about small beginnings. When the Angel of the Lord visits him, he's threshing wheat in a winepress - hiding food from Israel's enemy, the Midianites. Israel was given into the hands of their enemies by God after their continual disobedience and evil ways. Gideon is told that he will be a mighty warrior to defeat the Midianites and that God Himself would be with him. It's hard to believe news like this when your people are hiding from the enemy in caves. More than that, when you are the smallest clan of the smallest tribe of Israel, *what good can come out of Nazareth?*

It is when we are faced with circumstances out of our control, overwhelmed with our disqualifications, and fearful of the future that we question where God is. It's only natural to wonder this when we look at circumstances without spiritual eyes - looking to who we are and can see with rather than who God is and what He can do.

Shalom means *completeness, soundness, welfare,* and *peace,* The kind of peace Gideon experienced wasn't found in a lack of enemies, a solution to his problems, or a change in circumstance. *Gideon found a shalom transcendent upon any circumstance* - a wholeness in knowing that no matter what came his way, God was indeed with him. When storms of life hit, there is a peace no one can take from us when we remember that Jehovah Shalom is with us.

Praying Over the Promises of His Names

Jehovah Shalom,

You know me so well. You know all the problems I face, the pain held close to my heart, and the fearful thoughts that circle in my head. You already know the prayers I need answered, the miracles I'm yet to experience, and the future I will one day step into.

While I'm in this season of unknowns, questions, doubts, and fears, I choose to move from what I see with my eyes and turn to you. You created me, walk through each day with me, and wrote a book about each day of my life. You are the Author of my life - the loving Shepherd who keeps me safe - so I will hold fast in hope that you will continue to take care of me. Even if I walk through the valley of the shadow of death, I know you are with me, so I will fear no evil (Psalm 23:4). I will not forget all you have done for me!

When circumstances scream for me to hide away in fear, I choose to no longer cower to the fear of the world. I will _no longer_ let the lies of the enemy, the spirit of fear, have power in my mind or heart. I trust that you, Jehovah Shalom, are the ultimate peace and wholeness in my life. Even if everything around me fails, I know that you will always be with me, so I will cling to you with a firm foundation of hope despite what fear says! Anxiety does not have the final say. You do.

Ways to Make this Prayer Personal:	1	2	3
	Like Gideon, are there any lies you believe that disqualify you from being used by God?	Struggling with fear? Be honest with God and ask for an encounter with His perfect peace today!	List the ways God has taken care of you. Remembrance is powerful and removes doubt!

_____

_____

_____

_____

WEEK ONE RECAP

Reflect on His Promises

Take a few minutes to meditate on the names you've studied this week. In each box, reflect on times you've seen God's character in this way. If you have, jot down a testimony of Him keeping this promise. If you haven't, write down areas in your life where you want to see Himself shown in this way. Use the verse toolbox at the back of this resource to read more about the name of God and the promises they bring.

Elohim:
God the Creator;
Mighty One

El Roi:
The God who
Sees Me

Jehova Rapha:
The Lord
our Healer

Jehovah Jireh:
The Lord
our Provider

Jehovah Shalom:
The Lord is
our Peace

WEEK TWO

06 Yahweh Nissi: Lord is My Banner

> *"Moses built an altar there and named it Yahweh-Nissi, which means 'the Lord is my banner.'"* (Exodus 17:15)

Have you ever started a new season of your life, confident that it will be better than the last, only to find that it feels like it is worse than before? That's exactly how the Israelites felt after God took them from Egypt's slavery into the wilderness. While God had taken them from bondage, claiming them as His own, and provided for every need they had, we find the Israelites complaining once again about their situation as they prepare for battle.

"Why did He bring us here? We were better off before." Had they already gone back on the promise to remember the Red Sea? What forgetful people we are.

It's easy to think this way when all we know is what we saw before. How can we see what's coming our way? How can we trust that God has something more for us? We find ourselves wondering, *"I see you, God, I do, but is this really better than before?"*

In Exodus 17:7, right before our theme verse, there's another debacle for water and the Israelites question if this situation they find themselves in is better than what they once knew. Moses names the place *Massah* (test) and *Meribah* (arguing), because "the people of Israel argued with Moses and tested the Lord by saying, 'Is the Lord here with us or not?'"

After this, there is the famous battle with the Amalekites. Moses stands at the top of the hill holding his staff up for the entire battle (*arm day, amiright?*) as his people win.

Moses builds an altar named Yahweh-Nissi, the Lord is my banner. This was the first of many battles the Israelites would fight for their Promised Land. I'd like to believe the people sacrificing at the altar now knew the answer to their question - *the Lord truly was with them.*

As we enter new, uncertain seasons and are met with moments where our faith is tested, it is funny how we question where God is. It is as if our mind forgets all the victories God has won, the manna that fell from the heavens, or the impossible Red Sea that was parted for us to walk through.

When we cling tightly to God, our banner, we remind ourselves of more than the past; *we declare the future.* We hold fast to our identity as God's children, knowing we have a Father who is exclusively in the business of victory.

Just because we experience battles, uncertainty, or situations that seem worse than what we've seen before doesn't mean that our new season won't be better than before. When times are tough, Egypt may look like a better option, but as we recall that the Lord is with us and holds each victory in His hand, the presence of battles no longer makes us question if God is with us. We can be expectant, looking for God's victory to shine through.

The battles we go through aren't meant to be the bondage of Egypt again. Each moment of testing and faith are stones we can carry with us, building a place of remembrance we can come back to when we finally arrive in our Promised Land.

As we fixate on who He is: His character, word, and what He has already done for us - we can confidently hold onto Him as a banner of victory over us in any situation we face.

Praying Over the Promises of His Names

Yahweh Nissi,

I pray today for both present and future battles and ask that you would show yourself as my banner of victory. When I'm tempted to look back at the previous season and doubt your plan for good, encourage me to see the Promised Land ahead. Give me the boldness to not be swayed by what I see with my eyes and stand firmly on who you are.

Use these battles as opportunities to build a stronger faith in who you are and a deeper trust in the words you speak over me. May I never forget that you are with me always, even when my situations seem as if you are nowhere to be found. Thank you for every victory you bring my way. Thank you for the faithfulness that never leaves me - *I will fully lean upon you.*

Ways to Make this Prayer Personal:

✓ Are you still looking back at what was? We can't afford to hold onto the old! Take this moment to be honest with God and let go of what is holding you back. Repent for the ways you've held onto the past or complained about the new season He has brought you into. Ask for deeper faith to trust that He has only good plans for your life!

✓ Think about the places you've experienced Yahweh Nissi. Write the victories down and spend time thanking God for them. Display what you've written somewhere you'll see it often. Make this your own altar - a place of worship and remembrance for what God has done for you.

As we fixate on who He is: His character, word, and what He has already done for us - we can confidently hold onto Him as a banner of victory over us in any situation we face.

_____

_____

_____

_____

_____

07 Immanuel: God with Us

"**Look! The virgin will conceive a child! She will give birth to a son, and they will call him Immanuel, which means 'God is with us.'**" (Matthew 1:23)

From the beginning of time, *God knew*. The Creator of the Universe knew what would happen in the Garden of Eden, and that His Son would come to save the world from sin. This moment in Matthew 1 with Mary was planned - God wasn't caught by surprise that the world needed a Savior. From the start, it was planned that Jesus would come, equally as man and God, to pay the ultimate price so that we may be with Him forever.

It is because Immanuel came down to earth, paying this price over two thousand years ago, that we can walk daily with Him. We can personally know Jesus, both as God and as a human that struggled in all the ways we do - *thank you, Jesus, for that!*

Our relationship with God goes beyond El Roi, Him seeing and knowing us - we're invited to live a life of intimate communion with Immanuel, the One who walks daily with us. He understands our humanity because He was tempted in every way we are. *The things we're ashamed of do not scare Him away.* Coming as a humble servant - considering not His position as God to be used as an advantage (Philippians 2:6) - His name, Immanuel, reminds us of His endless love for us. It is a love that never stops pursuing us - so much so that even death could not keep us apart from Him.

From the beginning of time, God had a plan to save you - for you to live a life with Immanuel by your side.

Praying Over the Promises of His Names

Immanuel,

Sometimes I forget that you came to earth fully human. Too often, I think only of the miracles and power you displayed as the Son of God, forgetting the times when you were tempted and tested to obey the Father - *even when it was to death.*

I cannot imagine the level of sacrifice you gave in return for your Bride, the Church. *For me.* What a sacrifice it was to leave the Father - to leave perfect Heaven - and come down to a world filled with sin. Yet, you endured all of these things to become the God that walks with His people. You did not consider being God a position to use for an advantage. You chose a humble beginning so you could walk with me, so I could know you personally. How thankful I am to have a relationship with you, Immanuel.

When I'm faced with the struggles of life, please help me to remember that you are invested in what I'm going through - *you aren't passive or uncaring.* Remind me to invite you into each situation I face, knowing that I don't have to walk this path alone. You sacrificed it all because you *want* to walk it alongside me. Nothing is too big or too small for you to care about, so I will run to you, my beautiful Savior and best friend.

_____

_____

_____

_____

_____

08 Yahweh Tsuri: Lord is My Rock

"The LORD is my rock, my fortress, and my savior; my God is my rock, in whom I find protection. He is my shield, the power that saves me, and my place of safety." (Psalm 18:2)

Before David knew what it was like to be the King of Israel, he first learned what it was to be hidden from the world, running away from those trying to kill him - probably struggling to believe the things God spoke to him would come true.

David knew from personal experience that circumstances around us can change in a moment, but finding safety in Yahweh Tsuri is eternal. Unlike the rocks of this world that can break or shift, the Rock of our salvation - Jesus, our Cornerstone - is unmovable and constant. He is the eternal Rock (Isaiah 26:3-4).

When we understand that our safety in the Rock transcends anything we face in life, we can walk through anything with confident reassurance that we are not alone.

The key to experiencing Yahweh Tsuri is not simply saying a heartfelt "save me" prayer whenever you experience trouble. We are invited to live a life steady on the Rock by building our lives upon Him. In Matthew 7:24-27, Jesus teaches that without building upon Him, our firm foundation, anything we try to build will crumble the moment a storm comes.

As the storms of life hit, let us be prepared, having already built the foundation of our life upon Yahweh Tsuri. If we have Him, no storm can overtake us.

Praying Over the Promises of His Names

Yahweh Tsuri,

I can't control when the storms of life come, but what I can control is where I <u>choose</u> to run to. *Today, I choose to run to You, my strong fortress!*

I invite you into the storms of my life now and in the future. Please help me to build a firm foundation upon you, Jesus, that cannot shift as the world does. I put all of my trust in you, for I know that you will take care of me.

Teach me how to have unwavering hope, even when my eyes don't see the victory you have planned. I want to be content within You for however long my victory takes! Lord, I ask for forgiveness for all the times I have looked to the things around me for comfort - falsely trusting that something (or someone) can keep me safe other than you. You are the only one that satisfies. I am no longer content with sliding on other foundations - today is the day I decide to rest fully upon you, Yahweh Tsuri.

_____

_____

_____

_____

_____

_____

_____

09 Yahweh-Rohi: Lord is My Shepherd

"The Lord is my shepherd; I have all that I need." (Psalm 23:1-6)

Psalm 23 is a well-known psalm written by David, someone who knew what it meant to be both a sheep and a shepherd. This is a passage of Scripture that we can cling to in all seasons of our lives - a reminder that we are fully taken care of by our Shepherd.

As sheep, our job is easy: *listen to the Shepherd's voice* (John 10:27). You don't see sheep worrying about where they will sleep or what they will eat - in the same way, the Lord takes care of us as we follow Him closely (Matthew 6:33).

A shepherd's job was demanding. They were solely responsible for anticipating and providing for every need of their flock. They were devoted to the lives of the sheep, always on the lookout for potential dangers of wild animals and thieves. Each sheep was precious to them, and they dedicated their lives to shepherding daily. They were experts in the land surrounding them, knowing the locations of fresh water, shelter, and green pastures. They carried a rod and a staff to protect and discipline their beloved flock. This job was not easy or glamorous - the shepherd was willing to lay down his life daily for the well-being of his sheep.

Jesus is our Good Shepherd. He is the only One who can provide for us. As our Creator, He knows exactly what we need and when to provide it. As we fix our eyes on Him, keeping our ears open to hear His voice, we can fully rest in His protection - knowing that we lack nothing (Psalm 23:1). He knows well the terrain of our lives and leads us daily, dedicating Himself to our well-being.

For Jesus to be our Shepherd, we must submit ourselves as His sheep - recognizing our deep need for Him and committing to listening to His voice only. True sheep know the voice of the One who calls them by name. Even when they cannot see Him, they know His voice and obey it. They are unswayed by other shepherds around them; there is no confusion when it comes to knowing and obeying the voice of the One they follow.

The name Yahweh-Rohi comes with a promise. He will take care of you. He will love you. He will protect you. When you pass through dark valleys, He will walk alongside you. He will comfort you and provide rest for your weary soul.

When you strayed, the Good Shepherd left the ninety-nine to find you (Luke 15:4). He laid His life down so you can live a life under His covering - no longer in fear of your enemies or in want of anything. *All you have to do is rest in the promises of Yahweh Rohi, the Lord is my Shepherd.*

For Jesus to be our Shepherd, we must submit ourselves as His sheep - recognizing our deep need for Him and committing to listening to His voice only. True sheep know the voice of the One that calls them by name.

Praying Over the Promises of His Names

Yahweh Rohi,

You are my Shepherd, and I refocus my attention today on following you and *only you!* Holy Spirit, please teach me to hear my Shepherd's voice more clearly - to no longer confuse it with the other voices around me.

Teach me to be content in my current situation, having peace that surpasses all understanding because I fully trust that you are with me. When you are with me, I know that I will lack nothing, for you know exactly what I need and will not withhold things that are good from me. It is in your perfect timing that I am led to the green pastures. It is in your wisdom that my head is anointed with oil. It is your goodness and mercy, the *hesed* love of the Father, that follows me all the days of my life. I will confidently put all of my trust in you.

No matter how dark the valley is, I will fear no evil, for I know you are with me. I am hidden under the wings of your protection. Your loving-kindness sings over me and my soul is once again refreshed. Today, I take this moment to tell you how much I love you and how thankful I am that you laid your life down for me - the one out of the ninety-nine - who you did not leave on its own. And for this, I will follow you. I will put aside the other things vying for my attention and submit once again to your shepherding.

_____

_____

_____

_____

_____

_____

10 Jehovah Mekoddishkem: Lord Who Sanctifies

"'So set yourselves apart to be holy, for I am the Lord your God. Keep all my decrees by putting them into practice, for I am the Lord who makes you holy.'" (Leviticus 20:7-8)

The book of Leviticus covers many laws and ceremonial practices of the Levite priests. God emphasizes from the beginning of Israel's history that His people must remain pure and set apart - *holy as He is holy* (Leviticus 19:1). Jehovah Mekoddishkem (pronounced 'M-qadash'), is a name God calls Himself, which means 'the Lord who sanctifies you,' 'makes you holy,' or 'sets you apart as holy.' The Old Testament may simply look like restrictive religious rules; however, these decrees were created by God - filled with love, grace, and compassion - to help a people who could not attain holiness on their own become His chosen ones.

The world spreads a lie that there are many ways to be a "good person." We read obituaries of non-believers that celebrate charitable works, joyful hearts, and a positive effect on the world. And yet, no matter how "good" they were, if they didn't know Jesus (the New Covenant way to become holy), then they are not in Heaven. The reality is this: if we aren't followers of Jesus, we are not called a child of God; if we're not His child, the blood of Jesus cannot cleanse us of our sins to make us holy. Being a "good person" will never be enough - *it is only the blood of Jesus that sanctifies us, setting us apart as holy.*

The word holy is defined as a consecration for purification - *the way God keeps His people pure and sacred.* To be set apart is by keeping ourselves apart from unclean things, which is impossible to do on our own in a world filled with sin. The only way we can be made right with God is by becoming pure and holy - set apart from the sinful world around us. To be in the world but not of the world; is a miracle that is attained through Christ Jesus alone (1 Corinthians 1:30).

Jehovah Mekoddishkem, what a beautiful name - the loving, merciful God who sacrificed His only Son so that we could know what it means to be pure, holy, and set apart! We are now made right with God, empowered to live a life of holiness in every thing we do (1 Peter 1:15).

Praying Over the Promises of His Names

Jehovah Mekoddishkem,

It is in these moments that I am reminded of how sacred you are. It is easy to sing a song in church about your holiness, but it is another thing to humbly accept how short I fall of your standard. Though I try to be a "good person," it is humbling to be reminded that nothing I do is enough to meet your standard of holiness - *to be set apart and consecrated for you alone.*

In the Old Testament, the only way to be pure was to fulfill the decrees of the law - though it merely covered the problem for a time. Thank you, Jesus, for willingly paying the price of sin once and for all (Hebrews 10:10). Your blood washes over me and I am made new - a child of God set apart, filled with your Spirit, and consecrated as part of the royal priesthood (1 Peter 2:9). You fulfill your promise to sanctify us entirely and make us complete when we place our faith in you. Your grace fills in the gaps that I cannot reach, no matter how hard I try. *You are faithful to do as you promise* (1 Thessalonians 5:23-24).

_____

_____

_____

_____

_____

WEEK TWO RECAP

Reflect on His Promises

Take a few minutes to meditate on the names you've studied this week. In each box, reflect on times you've seen God's character in this way. If you have, jot down a testimony of Him keeping this promise. If you haven't, write down areas in your life where you want to see Himself shown in this way. Use the verse toolbox at the back of this resource to read more about the name of God and the promises they bring.

Yahweh Nissi: The Lord is my Banner	
Immanuel: God is with Us	
Yahweh Tsuri: The Lord is my Rock	
Yahweh - Rohi: The Lord is my Shepherd	
Jehovah Mekoddishkem: Lord Who Sanctifies	

These names of God reveal a power that many do not tap into - the testimonies and promises that are available to each one of us.

Verse Toolbox

I can write all about these names, but if you don't know where to look for these promises, the words I share won't accomplish much. If all you take from this study is a two-week devotional filled with written prayers you will never read again, *what use is it?* My prayer is that the words of this book are used by the Holy Spirit to touch your heart. But, more than that, my desire is for you to be equipped with the words God wrote for you! His words are LIFE - they hold power that we cannot imagine.

That is why I've included this toolbox. When you run into moments of doubt, fear, anxiety, and sadness - *when you question if God really is Jehovah Jireh, Shalom, or Rapha* - I want you to be equipped with the Truth. Look at these verses, read the stories of the people long before you who felt the same way, and take the promises for yourself. Cling to these verses and declare that you will see God this way too! If God did it for one of His children way back then, how much more would He do it again for you? His Words are the sword we battle our thoughts with. His Truth will overcome all fear and darkness, revealing His unfailing love and light to all those who seek Him!

Elohim	Genesis 1:1; 27, Jeremiah 29:11, Colossians 1:16, Ephesians 2:10, Revelation 4:11
El Roi	Genesis 16:13, Job 31:4, Psalm 33:18, Psalm 139:7, Isaiah 41:10, 1 Peter 3:12
Jehovah Rapha	Exodus 15:26, Psalm 147:3, Psalm 41:3, Jeremiah 17:14, Isaiah 53:5, 1 Peter 2:24
Jehovah Jireh	Genesis 22:13-14, Psalm 23:1, Matthew 6:33, Philippians 4:6; 19, Romans 8:32

Verse Toolbox

Jehovah Shalom	Judges 6:23-24, Psalm 23:4, Isaiah 26:3, John 16:33, Matthew 11:28-30, Philippians 4:7
Yahweh Nissi	Exodus 17:15, Deuteronomy 20:4, Psalm 3:8, Romans 8:37, 1 Corinthians 15:57, 1 John 5:4
Immanuel	Matthew 1:22-23, Genesis 28:15, Isaiah 7:14, Isaiah 9:6, John 1:14, Philippians 2:6
Yahweh Tsuri	Psalm 18:2, Psalm 19:14, 1 Samuel 2:2, Isaiah 26:3-4, Matthew 7:24-27
Yahweh Rohi	Psalm 23:1, Isaiah 40:11, John 10:11, John 10:27, Luke 15:4, 1 Peter 2:25
Jehovah Mekoddishkem	Leviticus 20:7-8, Exodus 31:12-14, Hebrews 10:10, John 17:17, 1 Thessalonians 5:23-24

My Notes

My Notes

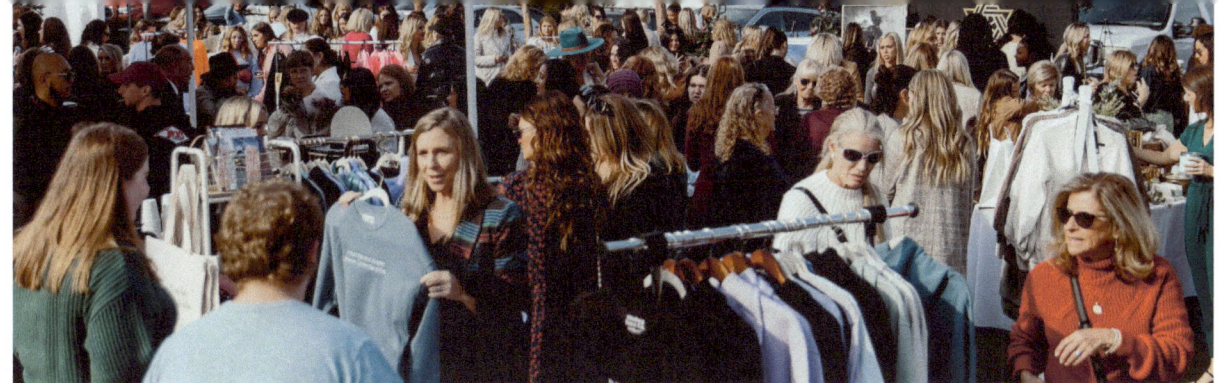

Hi, I'm Katie!

I never planned to start a business. After graduating, getting married, and surviving a pandemic, I had no clue what was next. But I knew God had a plan, so I spent the next year devoting my time to spending time in His Word, praying for my calling, and figuring out what it meant to abide in Christ.

In a huge leap of faith, I began Abiding Love Co. in 2021 with the mission to create faith-based apparel and accessories to create intentional conversations about Jesus and encourage the everyday believer to abide in God's love.

In November 2022, I launched my year-long passion project, *The Abide Guide: An Intentional Guide and Journal for Studying God's Word.* This is a special resource near and dear to my heart because its purpose is to encourage and equip women from all walks of life to read Scripture daily and boldly!

For this next season of Abiding Love Co., I'm excited to add helpful resources like this e-book that you can use to propel your abiding relationship with Jesus, the True Vine.

To learn more about my small business, access additional resources, and stay connected with me, check out the website at www.abidingloveco.com or find us at @abidingloveco on Instagram, Facebook, and Pinterest!

My prayer is that this resource, and all of our other resources, remind you to abide in His love today.

Katie Talpos

More Resources from
Abiding Love Co.

The Abide Guide: An Intentional Guide + Journal for Studying God's Word is the perfect place to start if you're looking for a customizable, self-paced guide to studying Scripture. Each Guide comes with access to an exclusive Kickstart group with a full month of passages, videos, and resources to get you started!

Are you tired, burnt out, and burdened? The truth is, our weary souls can only be recharged by the One who gives us rest. We were made to live lighter. Girl, Lay Your Burdens Down is a free 3-day mini study on Matthew 11:28-30 that will encourage you to drop your worries at the cross and find much-needed rest for your soul!

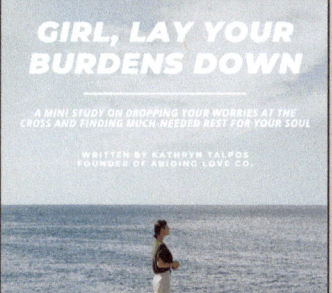

YES AND AMEN.

Yes and Amen: A Prophetic Word Journal is an intentional space for you to keep what the Holy Spirit is speaking to you in one place. The journal contains dedicated spaces for notes, key points and promises, Scripture passage references, personal application, prayer, and recorded testimonies!

Abiding Love Co. is a faith-based company offering apparel, accessories, resources, and more prayerfully made to create intentional conversations about Jesus and encourage believers to abide daily in the True Vine.

www.abidingloveco.com
@abidingloveco

NER - JEHOVAH SHALOM - THE LORD IS MY PEACE - ELOH
EATOR - EL ROI - THE GOD WHO SEES ME - IMMANUEL
S - YAHWEH TSURI - THE LORD IS MY ROCK - YAHWEH-R
S MY SHEPHERD - JEHOVAH MEKODDISHKEM - THE LC
FIES - EL ELYON - THE MOST HIGH GOD - EL OLA
TING GOD - EL SHADDAI - THE ALMIGHTY GOD - YAHWEH
RD OUR RIGHTEOUSNESS - JEHOVAH SHAMMAH - THE L
E - YAHWEH MACCADDESHEM - THE LORD YOUR SAN
SABBAOTH - THE LORD OF HOSTS - ATTIYQ YOUM - THE
JEHOVAH JIREH - THE LORD WILL PROVIDE - YAHWEH N
S MY BANNER - JEHOVAH SHALOM - THE LORD IS MY
- GOD THE CREATOR - EL ROI - THE GOD WHO S
UEL - GOD IS WITH US - YAHWEH TSURI - THE LORD IS M
-ROHI - THE LORD IS MY SHEPHERD - JEHOVAH MEKODDE
D WHO SANCTIFIES - EL ELYON - THE MOST HIGH GOD -
ERLASTING GOD - EL SHADDAI - THE ALMIGHTY GOD -
U - THE LORD OUR RIGHTEOUSNESS - JEHOVAH SHAMM
WHO IS THERE - YAHWEH MACCADDESHEM - THE LC
FIER - YAHWEH SABBAOTH - THE LORD OF HOSTS - ATTIY
CIENT OF DAYS - JEHOVAH JIREH - THE LORD WILL P
NISSI - THE LORD IS MY BANNER - JEHOVAH SHALOM -
EACE - ELOHIM - GOD THE CREATOR - EL ROI - THE GOD
IMMANUEL - GOD IS WITH US - YAHWEH TSURI - THE LO
YAHWEH-ROHI - THE LORD IS MY SHEPHERD -
DISHKEM - THE LORD WHO SANCTIFIES - EL ELYON - T
OD - EL OLAM - THE EVERLASTING GOD - EL SHADD
TY GOD - YAHWEH TSIDKENU - THE LORD OUR RIGHTEO
H SHAMMAH - THE LORD WHO IS THERE - YAHWEH MACCA
RD YOUR SANCTIFIER - YAHWEH SABBAOTH - THE LORD O
YOUM - THE ANCIENT OF DAYS - JEHOVAH JIREH - THE L
E - YAHWEH NISSI - THE LORD IS MY BANNER - JEHOVAH
RD IS MY PEACE - ELOHIM - GOD THE CREATOR - EL ROI -
ES ME - IMMANUEL - GOD IS WITH US - YAHWEH TSURI -
ROCK - YAHWEH-ROHI - THE LORD IS MY SHEPHERD
DISHKEM - THE LORD WHO SANCTIFIES - EL ELYON -
D EL OLAM THE EVERLASTING GOD EL SHADDAI

www.ingramcontent.com/pod-product-compliance
Lightning Source LLC
Chambersburg PA
CBHW041618120626
46551CB00003B/497